SILLY, SCRAPPY, SASSY HOLIDAY SONGS

Parodies of Christmas Pop Songs and Carols

Colorful Music Score Edition

Peter K Hainsworth

Score Arrangement: Arthur Brown

Illustration: Rodney Cooke

Cover design and illustrations by Rodney Cooke

All rights reserved. No part of this book may be reproduced in any form or by any means without permission in writing from the author.

TABLE OF CONTENTS

POP SONGS

Parody .... *Original*

1. Deck'd Our House .... Deck the Hall

2. Close to Home .... I'll be Home for Christmas

3. Let it Snow, Let it Snow .... Let it Snow, Let it Snow

4. Jangle Horns Chase Santa .... Jingle Bells

5. Sir Rudolph the Red .... Rudolph

6. Modern Christmas Times .... O Tannenbaum

7. Punk Rockers .... Santa Claus is Comin' to Town

8. Holly and Ivy .... The Holly and The Ivy

9. Holiday Ups and Downs .... Have Yourself a Merry Little Christmas

10. Mankind's Fantasies .... Here Comes Santa Claus

CAROLS

Parody .... *Original*

11. Sally, Me and a Kitten .... Away in a Manger

12. All Ye Consumers .... Oh Come All Ye Faithful

13. Ye Merry Couples .... God Rest Ye Merry, Gentleman

14. Jerusalem .... O Little Town of Bethlehem

15. Our New E-World .... Joy to the World

16. It's the Thought .... Hark! The Herald Angels Sing

17. Three Big-Wigs .... We Three Kings of Orient Are

18. Good Pres. Clinton .... Good King Wenceslaus

19. When'd it all Start .... The First Noel

GETTING THE MOST FROM THIS BOOKLET!

NOTE: EACH OF THE 19 SONGS HAS A LEFT AND RIGHT PAGE:

THE LEFT SIDE, HAS THE SCORED MUSIC AND LYRICS:
*for Those Who Read Music, the chord changes above the score
for the accompanist, can support the singers (as in a fake book).
At some point, it could be sung acapella:
*for Those Who Don't Read Music, the pianist can teach them
by banging out the melody in accompanying.

THE RIGHT SIDE HAS TWO USES:
a) THE PARODY LYRICS CAN BE RECITED AS A POEM,
in conjunction with the singing, before or after.

b) SINCE MANY SINGERS WILL KNOW THE ORIGINAL TUNES:
the Parody lyrics can be sung with their accompaniment; or even bolder,
sing the Original and the Parody versions one after the other -
to experience the way one takes off from the other to make a
contemporary comment.

WHY WRITE PARODIES TO THESE BELOVED SONGS?
Certainly not to supplant or denigrate them in any way.

I LOVE all the Holiday Pop Songs & Carols - sing them every chance I get:
at people's homes, in the car or at church....have for many decades.

However, starting at Thanksgiving, they blast on radio, TV, at Malls, everywhere.
After a while, it's too much and they lose their wonder. For fun, I decided to make
parodies of them: some Silly, some Salty (risqué), some Sassy...
all about our modern world at this season.

The tunes have been altered slightly to reflect the moods of the parodies.
Some of the original words appear so that the relationship is suggested.

IT'S ALL MEANT IN FUN. IF THE CONTENT OF A COUPLE OF SONGS-
BOTHER YOU - JUST SKIP THEM AND ENJOY THE OTHERS.
PKH

1. Deck'd Our House

[Spoken] SURE DISNEY WILL BUY AND INSTALL IT ALL!

1. DECK'D OUR HOUSE sing to the tune of DECK THE HALL (Boastful)

<u>1.</u> Deck'd our house with boughs of Holly: Fa la la la la, Fa la la la.
Lights, everywhere do look, so Jolly: Tra la la la la, Tra la, la la.

Many statues, front, side and rear, yeah: It's a gas, None do pass, Ya ya ya.
Traffic piles up for sixteen blocks: Ha ha ha ha ha, Ha ha ha ha.

<u>2.</u> Tunes are blaring, creatures rocks'n talks: Do re mi fa so, Bob to and fro. Santa, on the roof, with eight, reindeer: Whoa oa oa oa oa, whoa oa oa oa.

We can afford the Pow'r bill, Yes: Yo-ho-ho, Yo-ho-ho, Yo-ho-ho.
We will win the City's top a-ward: Just magnifico. What a great show!

[Speak] **MAYBE DISNEY WILL BUY AND INSTALL IT ALL!**

2. Close For Christmas

[Spoken] I'LL DEFINITELY COME FOR NEW YEAR'S, OR EASTER!

2. CLOSE TO HOME sing to the tune of I'LL BE HOME FOR CHRISTMAS (Lonesome)

<u>1.</u> Why is it stormy this Christmas? Snow drifts are piled up so high. The weather forecasts, they are so troubling. I surely hope I can fly.

<u>2.</u> The gifts that I mailed for you all...delivery may be tricky this year. Since not even a mouse can you get near your house, presents will late I do fear.

<u>3.</u> Did phone the airport, they won't promise, but they say come, it may clear. I just want to be with you so much now. I am trying hard to be near.

<u>4.</u> But now I am stuck at airport, I won't be getting out it seems. I'll phone, we'll talk, so I'll feel home for Christmas: if only in my dreams.

[Speak] **I'LL DEFINITELY COME FOR NEW YEAR'S OR EASTER!**

3. LET IT SNOW sing to the tune of LET IT SNOW, LET IT SNOW (Flippant)

Oh the chaos inside is frightful, but the outside looks so delightful. With relatives here in tow, there's no peace or calm 'til they go.

They don't show signs of leaving, the Kids and Adults are peeving. We turned the lights way down low, but they don't go, they don't go, all is woe.

When they finally say goodnight, how they hate going out in the storm. If we get them all really tight, all the way home they'll be warm.

The fire is starting to die, and the house looks like a pigsty. But when their gone we'll glow. Stay inside, be relax'd..... just LET IT SNOW.

[Speak] **MAYBE NO SCHOOL OR WORK FOR A WEEK, HURRAH!**

4. Jangle Horns

[Spoken] STOP THE PRESSES! HEAR THIS, HEAR THIS!

4. JANGLE HORNS sing to the tune of JINGLE BELLS (Boldly)

1. Dashing through the snow, in my soup'd-up modern sleigh. O'er the roads I go, just racing all the way.

Horns a dreadful honking, black smoke a-belching out. What fun to crash ten states, a thousand miles tonight, no doubt.

Oh! Jangle Horns, Jangle Horns, in a real fast cart, like a super-sonic dart.

2. Crashing thru the drifts, just like a big snowplow. I am looking up for Santa, he should be coming right now.

To see the reindeer prancing, oh that is what I crave. If he broadcasts, then I'll pick up his signal on shortwave.

And I will tell just everyone that he waved to me, on his trip 'cross land and sea.

[Speak] **STOP THE PRESSES! HEAR THIS, HEAR THIS!**

5. Sir Rudolph The Red

[Spoken] CASTLE ROOMS NOW FOR RENT: E-MAIL rudolph@redhose.com

5. SIR RUDOLPH THE RED — sing to the tune of RUDOLPH (with SILLY COMMENTS)

Sir Rudolph the Red he knows rain dears [R, AI N] and he really knows his snows [GOT SOAKING CLOTHES]. He sits on top of his huge castle [IT'S A HASSLE], in his red, so shiny hose [ANDA RED ROSE].

Behind his back the nasty courtiers, laughed and called him silly names. [LIKE LAME BRAIN] They never let Sir Rudolph play in courtly games [LIKE FREEZE FRAME].

Then one foggy Christmas Eve, Santa came to say [HEY OVER THERE]. Sir Rudolph with your hose so bright, you led my reindeers here tonight. [WE'RE SOME PAIR].

Then all the castle loved him, and they shouted out with glee. [KINDA PHON-EE]. Sir Rudolph the Red was so happy, [NOT SNUBBED, HAPPY] 'cause he went down in history. [IN HISTORY].

[Speak] **CASTLE SUITES NOW FOR RENT: CALL RUDOLPH@REDHOSE.COM**

6. Modern Christmas Times

Oh, Tan-en-baum, our Christ-mas tree, al-though you're fake, you're rea-lly fun. Right from a box with lights in-tact. You plug it in and then yer done. Your boughs were real in yes-ter year, but nee-dles dropped, was such a mess. O Tan-en-baum our Christ-mas tree, use a-gain next year, no stress. Un-der-neath the tree, the gifts you see, they're all for us so lov-er-ly. Kids ask for HOT new fan-cy toys, those sa-vy lit-tle girls and boys. So hea-ven help dear Mom and Dad, if the stores ran out, t'would be a crime. O Christ-mas time, a fran-tic time, but real-ly is, so su-blime.

[Spoken] SOME JEWISH FRIENDS THINK THE SEASON JOLLY TOO!

6. MODERN CHRISTMAS TIMES sing to the tune of O TANNENBAUM (Wistfully)

<u>1.</u> O Tanenbaum, our Christmas tree, although you're fake, your really fun. Right from the box with lights intact. You plug it in and then yer done.

Your boughs were real in yesteryear, but needles dropped was such a mess. O Tanenbaum, our Christmas tree: use again, next year, no stress.

<u>2.</u> Underneath the tree, the gifts you see, they're all for us so loverly. Kids will ask for HOT new fancy toys, those savvy little girls and boys.

So heaven help dear Mom and Dad, if the stores run out, would be a crime. O Christmas time, a frantic time, but really is, so sublime.

[Speak] **SOME JEWISH FRIENDS THINK THE SEASON JOLLY TOO!**

7. Punk Rockers

[Spoken] RUN FOR THE HILLS... YOU MAY BE SAFE THERE!

7. PUNK ROCKERS sing to the tune of SANTA CLAUS IS COMING TO TOWN (Dire Warning)

You better watch out, get ready to cry, don't get tickets, I am telling you why; Punk Rockers is coming to town.

They're screaming bad rap for their new world tour, with lyrics they get right from the sewer. Punk Rockers is coming to town.

They'll blast you in the concert at two hundred decibels. They'll take you for a devotee of their smut that just repels.

If you value your hearing and your sanity, don't just pout, protect your humanity. Don't let Punk Rockers steal 'way your soul, yes YOUR SOUL.

[Speak] **RUN FOR THE HILLS...YOU MAY BE SAFE THERE!**

8. Holly And Ivy

Oh Hol-ly and friend I-vy, both feet are on the ground. Hap-py in a house that is all their own. And no man to whom they are bound. They rise with the mor-ning sun shine, they go run-ning with the deer. Don't need use of the Mer-ry O or-gan; there are o-ther tools, have no fear. Nei-ther bared an in-fant blos-som, as white as li-ly flow-er. Can a-dopt a kid of just an-y col-or. Who can fight with fe-male po-wer? The ri-sing moon will find them ha-ving drinks with their cool friends. For the way they live is ac-cep-ted now: they are set-ting their own mo-dern trends.

[Spoken] THEY ARE HERE: LIFE GOES ON FINE, GET USED TO IT!

8. HOLLY AND IVY sing to the tune of THE HOLLY AND THE IVY ('HIP' Style)

<u>1.</u> Oh Holly and friend Ivy, both feet on the ground. Happy in a house that is all their own. And no man to which they're bound.

They rise with the morning sunshine, they go running with the deer. Don't need use of the Merry O-or-gan, there are other tools have no fear.

<u>2.</u> Neither bared an infant blossom, as white as a Lilly flower. Can adopt a kid of just any color; who can fight with female power?

The rising moon will find them having drinks with their cool friends. For the way they live is accepted now, they are setting their own modern trends.

[Speak] **THEY ARE HERE, LIFE GOES ON FINE: GET USED TO IT!**

9. Holiday Ups And Downs

[Spoken] SEEMS IT'S ALWAYS UNEQUAL, SHAME!

9. HOLIDAY UPS AND DOWNS — sing to the tune of HAVE YOURSELF A MERRY LITTLE CHRISTMAS
(Conflicting Emotions)

Christmas is all about merry expectations, being with your relations. But many gifts make your wallets light, with the bills that go out of sight, yah! And if you're Yuletides gay, you plan it just your way.

We all try to dodge sale crowds frantic push and lust: presents for all a just, must.

These days, abandoned souls will often get depressed, others with getting gifts, obsessed. Pity the stranded ones, poor or unemployed, their kids' scant hopes destroyed.

Suicide rates climb, from loneliness, I guess. Hospitals do a brisk business. Most get weary but full of hope and cheer. These bright holidays are the peak of every year.

[Speak] **SEEMS IT'S ALWAYS UNEQUAL, SHAME!**

10. Mankind's Fantasies

[Spoken] DIFUSE ALL WARS! SUPPORT ALL LIFE!

10. MANKIND'S FANTASIES sing to the tune of HERE COMES SANTA CLAUS (Earnestly)

<u>1</u>. Here comes Santa Claus, there go Santa Clauses, hundreds merry and bright. Reduce unemployment, increase kids enjoyment, that seems proper and right.

So we like this fantasy, him flying around the world, our childhood faith we retrieve. Now Jesus and Mohammed, they say, flew to their God: many miracles we're to believe.

<u>2</u>. But we're not children, sure life can be scary. We are all awed and afraid. So, many Gods raised high to intervene for believers: Spiritual, but just man-made: and many wars and atrocities, committed in the NAME.

Rather, fight for Human Rights: no oppression, starving, prejudice. This the creed to work for and acclaim.

[Speak] **WARS: RELIGIOUS, STATE OR TRIBAL ~ WE MUST DIFFUSE**

11. Sally, Me And A Kitten

[Spoken] WHEW! THAT WAS A CLOSE ONE!

11. SALLY, ME AND A KITTEN sing to the tune of AWAY IN A MANGER (Tongue-in-Cheek)

<u>1</u>. Away in a high manger, I met Sally Granger. A happening you will not find anywhere stranger. What were you two doing there is what adults did say, rolling around in the sweet smelling hay?

<u>2</u>. We kids just sought her kitten just FOUR weeks old. Oh please believe our story, so true and so bold. We sense none will believe it, call us sinners, maybe wuss. And blame us forever, not love us but fuss.

<u>3</u>. If that is your conclusion, we'll try to understand. We'll not get to heaven, be driven from the land. So decided just to tell the whole honest truth. The poor thing was really TEN not FOUR weeks old: we came down at once, forsooth.

[Speak] **WHEW, THAT WAS A CLOSE ONE!**

12. All Ye Consumers

[Spoken] MORE SPENDING, MORE JOBS, MORE SPENDING, DUH!

12 ALL YE CONSUMERS sing to the tune of
OH COME ALL YE FAITHFUL (Lighthearted)

1. Oh come all ye consumers, of your funds so wary. Know that in this economy spending is so scary.

But malls have many a gift, so loved ones will get a lift.
Oh! ogle things of beauty, buy lots and don't be snooty.
Oh! do your parts, save our blessed land: your civic duty.

2. So come all ye consumers. What's a little more debt, you might have to borrow funds or your house sublet. Worse, move in with the folks: you would suffer from silly jokes.

You, must, buy scads off the rack, Mack, to help the economy come back. Please don't wait for post-season sales, or return any in a sack, Jack. A-MEN

[Speak] **MORE SPENDING, MORE JOBS, MORE SPENDING, DUH!**

13. Ye Merry Couples

[Spoken] MARS AND VENUS!

13. YE MERRY, COUPLES sing to the tune of GOD REST YE MERRY, GENTLEMEN (Carefree)

<u>1.</u> So rest you merry Husbands now, no ballgames to delay.
Remember y'all, that sport is King on every holiday.
Deliver us to Satan's power, we want to go astray.

Oh, oh, tidings of easy lives and beer, the lads and beer.
Oh tidings of easy lives right here.

<u>2.</u> Busy Wives are settled in the kitchen where they like to be.
Just cooking, gabbing, catching up on gossip don't you
see? Know hubbies will be drunk as Lords, will we get
home safely?

Oh-ho, tidings of wondrous times for us, may take the bus.
Hope the day can end with no arguments or fuss.

[Speak] **MARS AND VENUS!**

14. Jerusalem

[Spoken] ANOTHER LINGERING PROBLEM FOR MANKIND!

14. JERUSALEM sing to the tune of O LITTLE TOWN OF BETHLEHEM (Sadly)

<u>1.</u> Oh Little town of Jerusalem, how rift we do see thee lie. Above that thy sad and restless sleep, the silent Rockets fly.

And in thy dark streets hideth, everlasting hate and fright. Religious wars from years ago, are harbored there tonight.

<u>2.</u> It's happened many times o'er the years, always bringing death and gore. The Moor and Christian, then the Cath'lic/ Protestant wars have left unhealed sores.

The slaughter of-and-by creeds, clans, skin tones gives a sickening chill. And peace on earth evades us still, when strife o'ercomes goodwill.

[Speak] **ANOTHER LINGERING BLIGHT ON MANKIND'S BEST HOPE**

15. Our New E-World

[Spoken] CONTINUOUS JOY TO THE WORLD, HOPEFULLY!

15. OUR NEW E-WORLD sing to the tune of JOY TO THE WORLD (Trepidation)

1. Joy to the world, Internet does sing. For Earth a glorious fling. Let every modern be-e-ing, prepare for this new spri-i-ing.

So people and businesses boom, in the city or in a tomb. It's essential, consequential, for us all to bloom.

2. Computers rule the world, with celestial speed. But hackers we must heed. The workforce may have problems when, robots suck up jobs, then.

And privacy much at risk, then your identity fades away. Conversation and reading paper books, will that be all.... passé?

[Speak] **CONTINUOUS JOY TO THE WORLD, HOPEFUL!**

16. It's The Thought

[Spoken] ANYWAY, WE'D REAL-LY ALL LIKE TO SAY... AND BELIEVE THAT!

16. IT'S THE THOUGHT sing to the tune of HARK! THE HERALD ANGELS SING (Very Silly)

Hark! the Advertisers sing. I gave my love a bagel Ring.
She then looked and said: All for me? Took a small bite out of the thing.

With pressure from Ad-men's slick drawl, she bought me a soccer ball. But when I try running, I trip and fall. So exchanged it at the mall.

2. Feeling guilty about that ball, gave my love a kewpie doll.
She stuck pins in it I recall, wooing a boy from East Bengal.

Seems the givers get confused. These receivers not amused.
Before all gift giving you denounce, it's the thought that really counts.

[Speak] **WE'D REA-LLY ALL LIKE TO SAY... AND BELIEVE THAT!**

17. Three Big-Wigs

[Spoken] THE WORLD CAN'T TAKE CONTINUING CHAOS AND REFUGEES.

17. THREE BIG-WIGS sing to the tune of WE THREE KINGS (Pained and Fearful)

1. We three Big Wigs of Orient are. Best seen and heard from very afar. Sunni and Shi-ite and Christian in conflict. It is all highly bizarre.

Just a hell of bombing, starving, gassing. Awesome displays of anger and might. With the Islamic State, Israel, in the midst, oh where's the light?

2. Arabia's Sauds bought Sunnis for years. Syria's Assad has caused trillions of tears. Iran's Shiite Clerics are Persian Empire vowed. Jordan's Hussein must go with the crowd.

Now Europe is swamped, by the refugees, that rush from spreading tyrannies. All together it's an affright, this explosive tragedy. Syrians, Africans, Balkanites fleeing West or lost at sea.

[Speak] **THE WORLD CAN'T TAKE MUCH MORE CHAOS AND REFUGEES!**

18. Good Pres. Clinton

[Spoken] NASTY USELESS PARTISAN STRIKES!

18. GOOD PRES. CLINTON sing to the tune of GOOD KING WENCESLAUS (Regretful)

<u>1</u>. Good Pres. Clinton lost...looked out on impeachment Monday. Joyful Republicans lay in wait, primed to block his pathway.

Brightly shone the camera lights, the ambient frost was cool. When a sure man, Ken Starr, came gathering withering fu-u-el.

<u>2</u>. Shoulda told it straight with remorse. Yonder luscious was after you. The issue is: should Congress be side-tracked by an ugly, long, partisan hullaballoo?

You're presidential, tireless works beam bright. You're still involved today. Ten thousand times more important, than an Apolitical, Personal Way-lay.

[Speak] **NASTY USELESS PARTISAN STRIKES!**

19. When'd It All Start?

[Spoken] HISTORIC SPIRITUAL, MODERN SCIENTIFIC... WHATEVER!

19. WHEN'D IT ALL START? sing to the tune of THE FIRST NOEL (Open Minded)

1. There was Adam and his Eve, so the Bible does say.
The first Man and Woman in the Eden's garden did play.
'Til a very friendly snake said an Apple partake.
God was angry said you're expelled from this 'zero' date.

2. So they left with their clothes on their backs and went out, to the desert, had fam'ly and wandered about. Later, populations skyrocketed, mankind much multiplied, 'spite wars, storms and famine, a most rocky ride.

3. Now science does tell us that our planet spun out six million years ago, when the whole universe erupted, with the Big Bang's mighty blow.

[Speak] **HISTORIC SPIRITUAL, MODERN SCIENTIFIC....WHATEVER!**

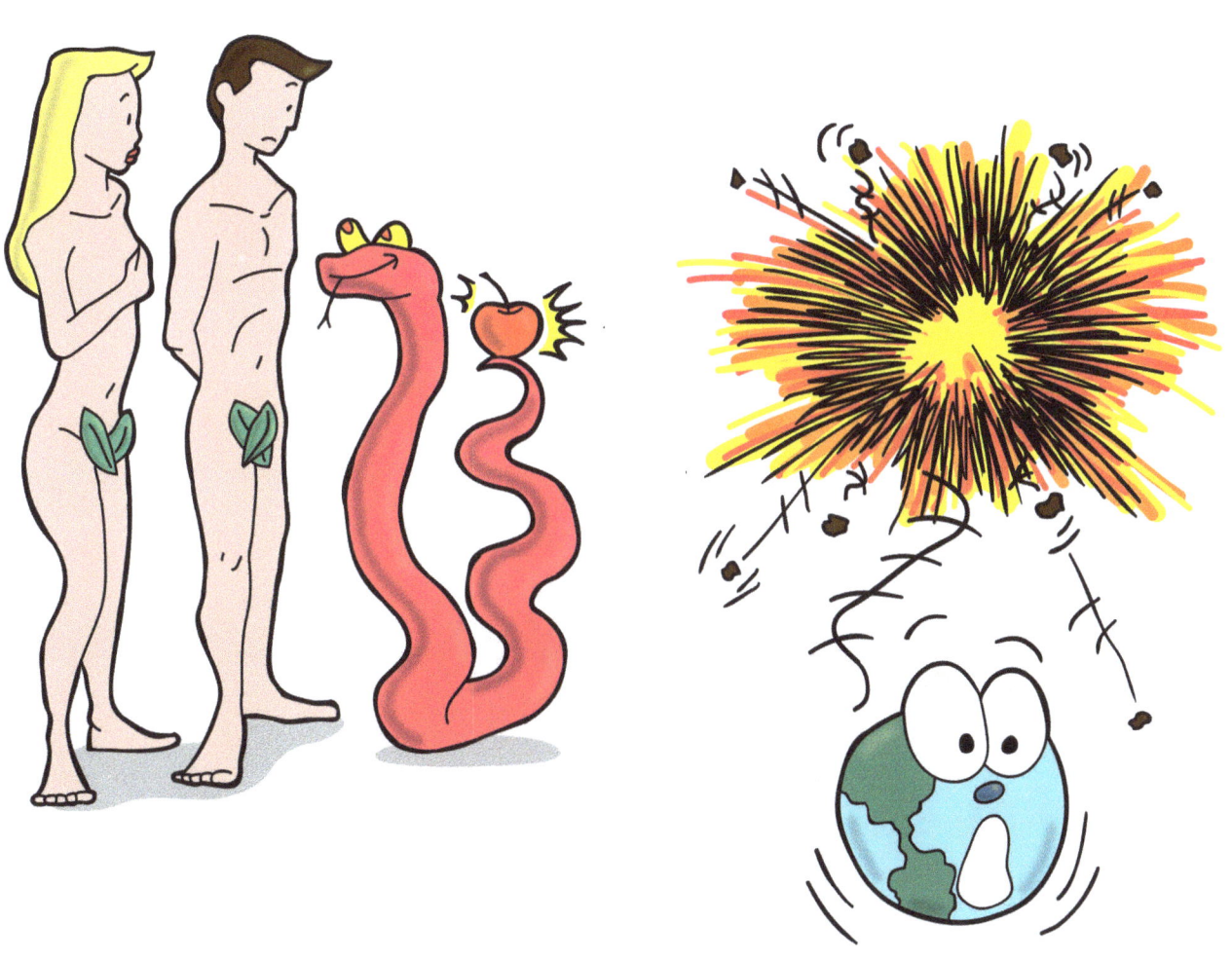

www.ingramcontent.com/pod-product-compliance
Lightning Source LLC
Chambersburg PA
CBHW051249110526
44588CB00025B/2932